Cutout Quilts

by Joyce Mori

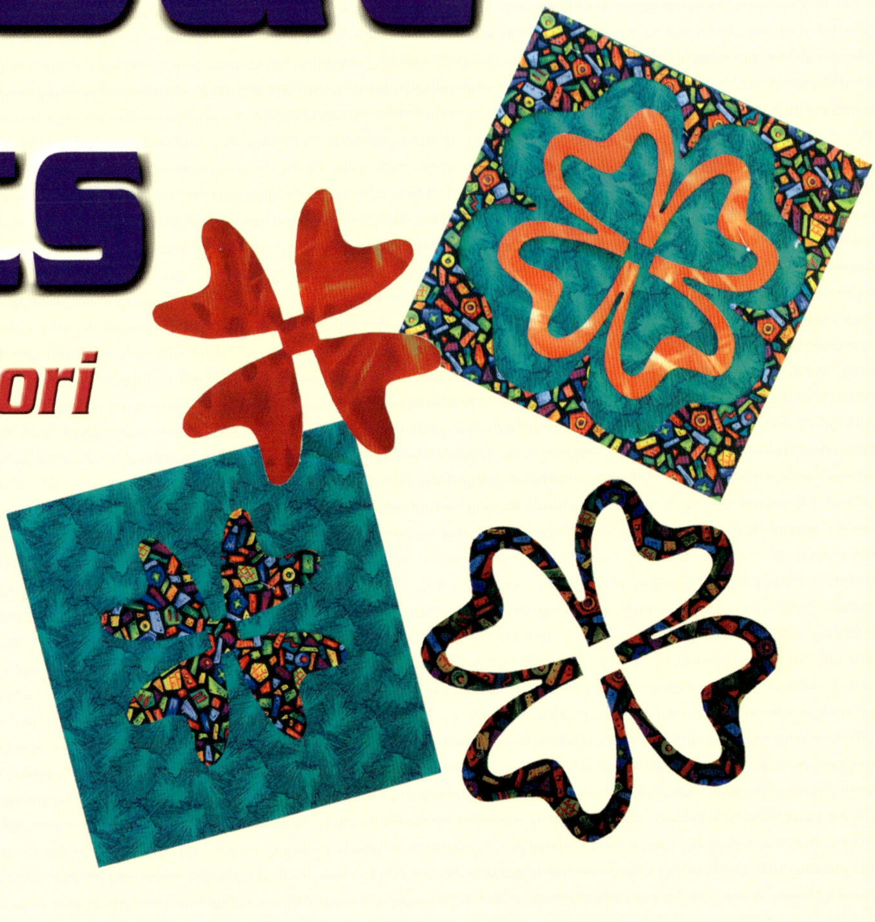

www.QuiltTownUSA.com

Copyright ©2003 Joyce Mori

All Rights Reserved.
Published in the United States of America.
Printed in China

Chitra Publications
2 Public Avenue
Montrose, Pennsylvania 18801-1220

No part of this publication may be reproduced or transmitted in any form or by any means, electronic or mechanical, including photocopy, recording, or any information storage and retrieval system now known or to be invented, without permission in writing from the publisher, except by a reviewer who wishes to quote brief passages in connection with a review written for inclusion in a magazine, newspaper, or broadcast.

First Printing: 2003

Library of Congress Cataloging-in-Publication Data

Mori, Joyce.
    Cutout quilts / by Joyce Mori.
               p.cm.
    ISBN 1-885588-50-X
    1. Patchwork — Patterns. 2. Patchwork quilts. I. Title.

TT835.M6819 2003
746.46'041—dc21
                                      2002155822

Edited by ... ...Elsie Campbell and Debra Feece
Design and Illustrations ... ...Brenda Pytlik
Photography ... ...Van Zandbergen Photography,
                                           Brackney, Pennsylvania

Introduction

Most of us like to see an advertising coupon that offers "two-for-one." The quilt blocks in this book offer quilters a two-for-one concept. When cutting the appliqué pieces for one block, you will be cutting pieces for a second one simultaneously. No fabric is wasted. And if you cut three layers of fabric at one time, you will have enough pieces for 6 blocks from one cutting.

My concept takes advantage of the idea of positive/negative images. For example, if you cut a circle from one square of fabric and appliqué it onto another, you have one block. The square from which you cut the circle can then be appliquéd onto another square of fabric, creating a second block with a circle in the center.

For the projects in this book, I chose to incorporate a wide range of fabric styles—brights, seasonal, calicoes, geometrics, batiks, etc. I tried to choose designs with different themes and to take into account different skill levels. There is something for everyone. I hope you enjoy making cutout quilts.

Acknowledgements

I want to thank my pattern testers Susan Miltenberger of Morgantown, West Virginia, Susan Marsh of West Allis, Wisconsin, and Pat Hill of West Hills, California, for helping me perfect the directions for the cutout quilt technique and for providing some of the quilts for this book.

Contents

Basic Steps to Making Cutout Quilts _____ 4

Embroidery Stitches _____ 6

Butterflies _____ 7

Power Flowers _____ 10

Casey's Friends _____ 12

Starfish in the Lagoon _____ 14

Hearts _____ 16

Curvaceous Squares _____ 18

Zigzag _____ 20

Flower Garden _____ 22

Giraffes on Parade _____ 24

Jagged Edges _____ 26

Bonus Block Designs _____ 31-32

Basic Steps to Mak

This book provides directions for 10 quilts and 3 special bonus designs! You do not have to use the colors I've selected for my quilts. Choose your favorite colors. If you would like a larger quilt, simply add additional blocks. For a smaller project, make fewer blocks.

First, select your fabrics. Yardage is based on 44"-wide fabric with a useable width of 42". All the background squares may be cut from the same fabric or from several different prints. Study the quilt photos for ideas. Be careful when selecting fabrics for the appliqué pieces. Dark backgrounds may shadow through light fabrics placed on top of them. Test for shadowing by placing your choice for appliqué pieces against the background fabric to make sure the background does not show through. If it does, you may wish to select a different set of fabrics. I like to use a variety of fabrics for both the appliqué pieces and the background squares to add more interest to the design.

There are two basic styles of blocks in these quilts and the simple drawings below illustrate them. In Style 1 the background block and the appliqué block are the same size. Begin by drawing a circle on a square of fabric that has been backed with fusible webbing. Carefully cut the circle out of the fabric. You have 2 pieces. The circle and the square that the circle was cut from so be careful to preserve both pieces. Each piece has a letter. The purpose of this is apparent when you read the detailed directions on page 5.

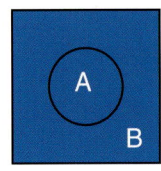

Separate the two pieces and place each of them onto additional squares of background fabric. Fuse them in place. Appliqué them to the background square. You have created two positive/negative image blocks, one with a dark square with a circle of the background fabric in the center, and the other with a square of background fabric with a dark circle in the center.

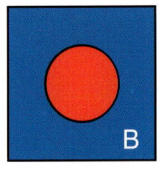 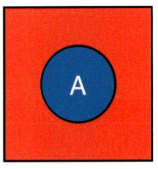

To make several blocks at once, layer two pieces of appliqué fabric together prior to cutting. This process will result in 4 separate appliqué pieces.

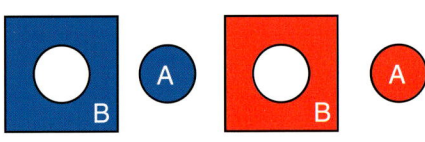

Style 2, Bordered Cutouts, involves extending the design options by placing each of the positive and negative cutouts on larger background blocks.

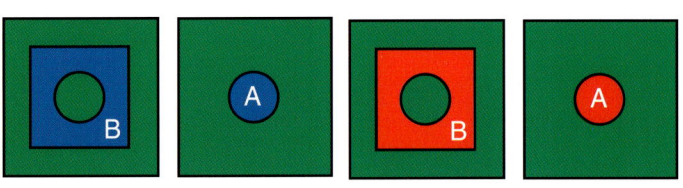

This gives the effect of borders on the blocks. As the cutout pieces become more complex, the design sophistication increases.

Getting started

- *Cut squares of fabric, fusible web, and stabilizer.*

After you've selected your fabrics, cut the appliqué and background squares. They should be cut to the size required for the project. Cut the squares of fusible web the same size as the appliqué squares. Then cut pieces of tear-away stabilizer the same size as the background squares.

ing Cutout Quilts

Adhere the paper-backed fusible web square to the wrong side of the appliqué squares, following the manufacturer's instructions. Remove the paper backing when it has cooled.

- *Cut the appliqué pieces.*

Enlarge the pattern to the correct size. Trace the appliqué design onto thin paper or photocopy it onto thin typing paper or tracing paper at a copy center. Tracing paper is slightly easier to use for this process than typing paper. The number of copies needed for each quilt is stated in the pattern. I allow one extra.

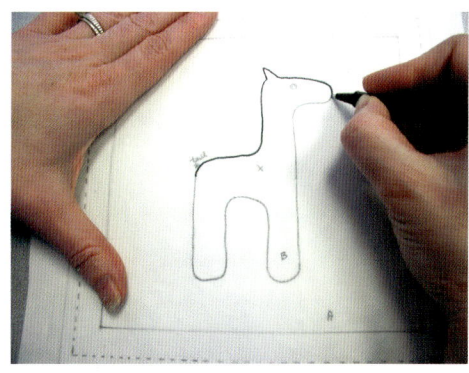

Layer two or three prepared appliqué squares, right sides up. NOTE: *It is not advisable to cut more than 3 layers at once. More than 3 layers of fabric with a fusible backing are difficult to cut accurately, as the layers tend to slip under the blades of the scissors.* I like to use a basting spray to hold the layers together. Pin and spray baste a pattern copy to the layered squares. Even if you've used the basting spray, place a couple pins through the layers to be sure nothing slips. There is an X on each pattern that marks the center of the block to use when you trace a pattern. If in the copying process your block looses a border just center the pattern, using the X, on your appliqué fabrics before you cut.

Using very sharp scissors, cut through all layers exactly on the pattern lines. If design lines go off the edge of the square, begin cutting at the edge. If the design requires that shapes be cut from the center of the squares, make it easier to insert your scissors by cutting a 1/2" to 1" slit along a pattern line with a small rotary cutter.

Label the pieces "A" or "B", according to the appliqué pattern. For each square, the pieces with letter A are placed on one background. Those with letter B are placed on another background.

- ***Fuse the appliqué pieces onto background squares.***

Once the pieces are cut, layer them on the background squares. Depending on the size of the quilt, I like to lay all the background squares out on a table, floor, or design wall. Place the "A" and "B" pieces on the background squares. You will have several pieces of the same shape in different colors. Mix the colors any way you wish. In fact, I think the more you vary the color, the more interesting your final quilt design becomes. Place an A piece on a background and on a B piece on another background. Do this until you have each of the pieces on a background. (Thank you, Sue Miltenberger, for the idea of lettering the pieces.)

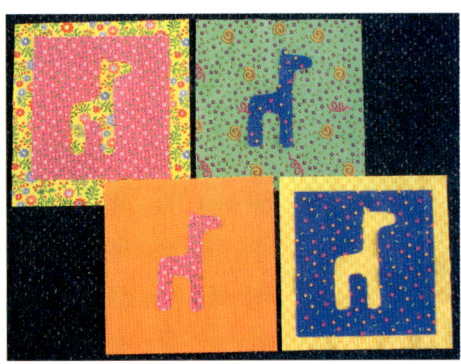

Use the cutout pattern pieces to help you center the pieces. If you are putting A pieces on a background, use the paper templates from cutting out the B pieces to help you space the appliqués. Refer to the original pattern to position the pieces on the background blocks.

When you are satisfied with your blocks, tack a couple of corners down with a mini-iron, or pin the pieces in place before moving them to the ironing board for the next step. Fuse the appliqué pieces in place, following the manufacturer's instructions.

- ***Appliqué the blocks.***

Practice your appliqué stitch on scrap fabric with stabilizer. Set your machine to your choice of small zigzag or blanket stitch. Check your machine's manual for any adjustments or settings.

When you are satisfied with the practice piece, you are ready to begin stitching on the quilt blocks. Layer a prepared block right side up on a block-sized square of tear-away stabilizer. Stitch the appliqué pieces in place.

NOTE: *If you are not familiar with machine appliqué, you may wish to consult your sewing machine dealer for further instructions. If your stitch is not perfect, there may be a burr on the throat plate or hook, or the machine's timing may be slightly off. Your dealer can check this out for you. It is also a good idea to install a new needle before beginning any project. Consider purchasing pre-wound bobbins as they hold more thread than ones you wind yourself. The color of thread you select for the machine appliqué is a matter of personal choice. You may select a color that emphazies the design or one that blends with the design.*

Measure the finished blocks. You may find it necessary to trim the blocks slightly so that they are all the same size before setting them together. Follow each pattern's directions for sashings and borders to complete the quilt top.

Embroidery Stitches

Lazy Daisy (Flower)

After knotting the thread, bring the needle up at A and down at B. B should be very close to A. Form a loop with the thread. Bring the needle up at C and through the loop. Anchor the loop by stitching down at D.

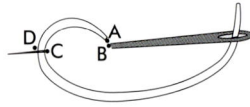

For a flower, make four Lazy Daisy stitches, as shown. Each stitch should be about 1/2" long.

Outline or Stem Stitch

Outline stitches give emphasis to blocks, or form new design lines in the quilt blocks. After knotting the thread, bring the needle up at A. Stitch down at C, bringing the needle up between A and C at B. The distance between points A and C should not be longer than 3/16".

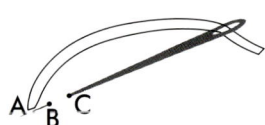

For the second stitch, go down at D and bring the needle up at C, and so on. I find it best not to bring the needle up in exactly the same hole as where it went down. Stay a thread or two away from the exact hole. Work the stitches along the line as shown on the pattern.

Satin Stitch

This is used for the dog's mouth in "Casey's Friends." After knotting the thread, bring your needle up at A and down at B and then up at C, and so on, filling the area marked on the pattern.

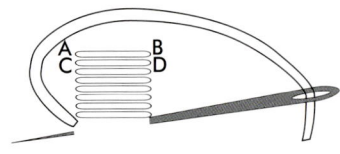

Butterflies

Lively diagonal lines give flight to your fancy!

Bright and beautiful, these butterflies will lighten the heart of young and old alike. **"Butterflies"** *takes a bit of a twist with candy cane-like striped sashing and borders.*

QUILT SIZE: 33" square
BLOCK SIZE: 7" square

MATERIALS
- 5 assorted bright prints, each at least 7 1/2" square, for the appliqués
- 9 assorted light to medium prints, each at least 7 1/2" square, for the background squares
- 1/4 yard red solid for the sashing stripes
- 1/2 yard white tone-on-tone print for the sashing and borders
- 1/4 yard blue mottled print for the outer border stripes
- 1/4 yard dark blue mottled print for the binding
- 1 1/8 yards backing fabric
- 37" square of batting
- Paper backed fusible web
- Tear-away stabilizer
- 3 pattern copies (See *Basic Steps to Making Cutout Quilts* on page 4.)
- Basting spray

CUTTING
Enlarge the pattern by 200%. Dimensions given include a 1/4" seam allowance.

For the appliqués:
Prepare the following squares for this Style 1 project with the fusible web as described in Basic Steps to Making Cutout Quilts *on page 4.*
- Cut 5: 7 1/2" squares, assorted bright prints

For the block backgrounds:
- Cut 9: 7 1/2" squares, light to medium prints, for the background squares

For the sashing:
- Cut 12: 2 1/2" x 4 1/2" rectangles, red solid
- Cut 24: 2 1/2" squares, white tone-on-tone print
- Cut 16: 2" x 2 1/2" rectangles, white tone-on-tone print
- Cut 4: 2 1/2" x 5 1/2" strips, white tone-on-tone print

For the inner border:
- Cut 2: 2" x 25 1/2" strips, white tone-on-tone print
- Cut 2: 2" x 28 1/2" strips, white tone-on-tone print

For the outer border:
- Cut 48: 2 1/2" squares, white tone-on-tone print
- Cut 1: 5 3/4" square, white tone-on-tone print
- Cut 1: 5 3/4" square, blue mottled print
- Cut 2: 2 1/2" squares, blue mottled print
- Cut 24: 2 1/2" x 4 1/2" rectangles, blue mottled print

Also:
- Cut 4: 2 1/2" x 44" strips, dark blue mottled print, for the binding
- Cut 9: 7 1/2" squares of tear-away stabilizer

DIRECTIONS
- Referring to *Basic Steps to Making Cutout Quilts* (page 4) make 9 Butterfly blocks.
- Remove the stabilizer.

For the striped sashing:
- Draw a diagonal line from corner to corner on the wrong side of each 2 1/2" white print square.
- Place a marked square on a 2 1/2" x 4 1/2" red solid rectangle, right sides together. Stitch on the drawn line, as shown. Make 12.

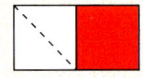

- Press the square toward the corner, aligning the edges. Trim the seam allowances to 1/4". Make 12.

- Place a marked square on the other end of a red solid rectangle. Stitch on the marked line. Press and trim, as before, to complete a pieced rectangle. Make 12.

- Stitch a 2" x 2 1/2" white print rectangle to each end of a pieced rectangle to make a vertical sashing. Make 6.

- Lay out 3 pieced rectangles, two 2 1/2" x 5 1/2" white print strips, and two 2" x 2 1/2" white print rectangles, as shown. Stitch them together to make a horizontal sashing. Make 2.

QUILT ASSEMBLY

- Referring to the quilt photo for placement, lay out the Butterfly blocks in 3 rows of 3 alternately with the vertical sashings.
- Stitch the blocks and vertical sashings into rows.
- Join the block rows and horizontal sashings.
- Stitch the 2" x 25 1/2" white print strips to the top and bottom of the quilt.
- Stitch the 2" x 28 1/2" white print strips to the sides of the quilt.

For the outer border:

- Draw diagonal lines from corner to corner on the wrong side of the 5 3/4" white print square. Draw a horizontal and a vertical line through the center.
- Place the marked square on the 5 3/4" mottled blue square, right sides together. Stitch 1/4" away from the diagonal lines on both sides.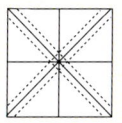
- Cut the square on the marked lines to yield 8 pieced squares. Press the seam allowances toward the blue. Set them aside.
- Make 12 pieced rectangles, as before, using twelve 2 1/2" x 4 1/2" blue mottled rectangles and twenty-four 2 1/2" white print squares.
- In the same manner, make 12 reverse pieced rectangles using the remaining 2 1/2" x 4 1/2" blue mottled rectangles and 2 1/2" white squares.
- Lay out 2 pieced rectangles, as shown. Sew them together to make a border unit. Make 12.

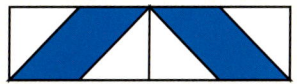

- Lay out 3 border units and 2 pieced squares, as shown. Stitch them together to make an outer border. Make 4.

- Stitch 2 outer borders to the sides of the quilt, referring to the quilt photo for orientation.
- Stitch a 2 1/2" mottled blue print square to opposite ends of the remaining outer borders. Stitch them to the remaining sides of the quilt.
- Quilt as desired and use the 2 1/2" x 44" dark blue mottled strips for the binding.

Pattern for Butterflies
(Enlarge by 200%)

Power Flowers

Reminiscent of the '70s, this flower motif is charming.

*Sue Miltenberger chose traditional looking fabrics for this attractive rendition of **"Power Flowers".** Her color choices are warm and rustic. Couched threads in the sashings create vertical and horizontal design lines that contribute a touch of class. The chenille yarn on the quilt below was twisted slightly into a bunch of three yarns and couched down. These quilts show how the same design can appear different depending on the fabric selection.*

QUILT SIZE: 41 1/2" square
BLOCK SIZE: 10 1/2" square

MATERIALS
- 1/2 yard each of navy, rust, beige, floral, and gold prints
- 1/2 yard light tan print for the sashing and border squares
- 1/3 yard navy print for the binding
- 1 1/3 yards backing fabric
- 48" square piece of batting
- Paper backed fusible web
- Tear-away stabilizer
- 3 pattern copies (See *Basic Steps to Making Cutout Quilts* on page 4.)
- Basting spray

CUTTING
Enlarge the pattern by 200%. Dimensions given include a 1/4" seam allowance.

For the appliqués:
Prepare the following squares for this Style 1 project with the fusible web as described in Basic Steps to Making Cutout Quilts *on page 4.*
- Cut 5: 11" squares, assorted navy, rust, beige, and gold prints

Also:
- Cut 9: 11" squares, assorted navy, rust, beige, and gold prints, for the background squares
- Cut 12: 2 3/4" x 11" strips, assorted navy, gold, beige, rust, and floral prints, for the border
- Cut 6: 2 3/4" x 36 1/2" strips, light tan print, for the vertical sashings
- Cut 6: 2 3/4" x 11" strips, light tan print, for the horizontal sashings
- Cut 12: 2 3/4" squares, light tan print, for the cornerstones
- Cut 4: 2 1/2" x 44" strips, navy print, for the binding
- Cut 9: 11" squares of tear-away stabilizer

DIRECTIONS
- Referring to *Basic Steps to Making Cutout Quilts* (page 4), make the 9 Power Flowers blocks.
- Remove the stabilizer.
- Referring to the quilt photo for placement, lay out the Power Flowers blocks in 3 vertical rows of 3, alternately with the 2 3/4" x 11" light tan horizontal sashings. Place the 2 3/4" x 36 1/2" light tan vertical sashings between the rows.
- Stitch the blocks and horizontal sashings into rows. Join the rows and vertical sashings to make the quilt top.
- Lay out three 2 3/4" x 11" border strips alternately with two 2 3/4" light tan print squares. Stitch them together to make a pieced border. Make 2.
- Stitch the pieced borders to opposite sides of the quilt.
- Lay out three 2 3/4" x 11" border strips alternately with four 2 3/4" light tan print squares. Stitch them together to make a pieced border. Make 2.
- Stitch the pieced borders to the remaining sides of the quilt.
- Finish the quilt as described in the *Basic Steps…*, using the 2 1/2" x 44" navy print strips for the binding.

Pattern for Power Flowers
(Enlarge by 200%)

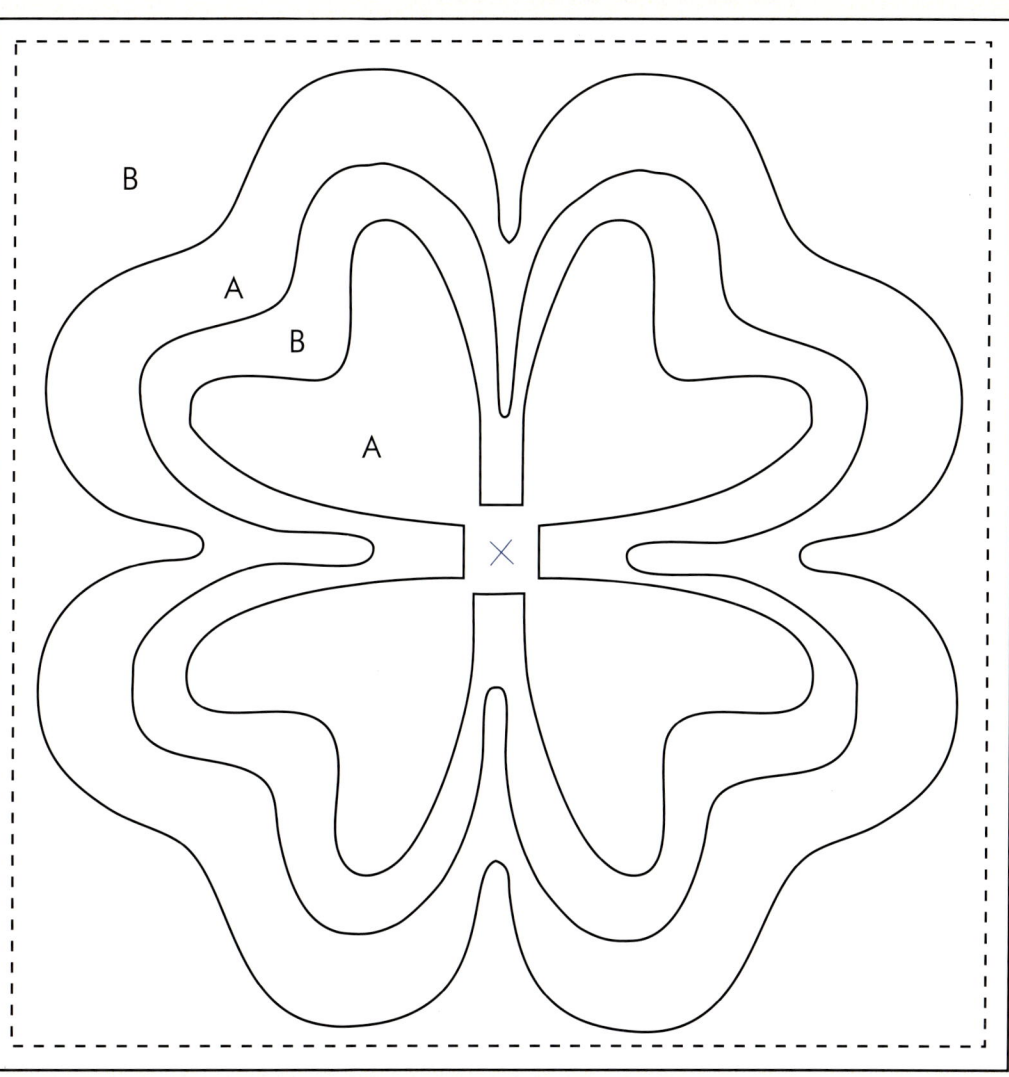

Casey's Friends
Puppy dogs make perfect pals for this cutout quilt!

Our daughter Susan has an adorable Norfolk Terrier named Casey that is affectionately known as my "granddog." I designed this quilt in honor of Casey and his furry friends. **"Casey's Friends"** *would make a perfect wall quilt for a child's room.*

QUILT SIZE: 25 1/2" x 29"
BLOCK SIZE: 7 1/2" square

MATERIALS

- 5 assorted tan to brown prints each at least 6 1/2" square, for the appliqués
- 9 assorted beige to brown prints, each at least 8" square, for the background squares
- 2" square of black solid, for the eyes
- 1/4 yard beige print, for the sashing
- 1/2 yard dark brown solid, for the bone appliqués, border, and binding
- Scraps of a puppy dog print with at least 6 motifs for appliqués
- 1 yard backing fabric
- 35" square of batting
- Red, beige, and several shades of brown embroidery floss
- Paper backed fusible web
- Tear-away stabilizer
- 3 pattern copies (See *Basic Steps to Making Cutout Quilts* on page 4.)
- Basting spray

CUTTING

Enlarge the pattern by 200%. Dimensions given include a 1/4" seam allowance.

For the appliqués:

Prepare the following squares for this Style 2 project with the fusible web as described in Basic Steps to Making Cutout Quilts *on page 4.*

- Cut 5: 6 1/2" squares, assorted tan to brown prints
- Cut 18: eyes (pattern on page 29), dark brown solid (NOTE: *Apply the fusible web to the wrong side of a small amount of dark brown solid as for the appliqué square before cutting the pieces from it.*)
- Cut 4: bones, dark brown solid (See note above.)
- Cut 6: Puppy dog motifs (NOTE: *Apply fusible web, as before, to fabric before cutting out the motifs.*)

Also:

- Cut 2: 2 1/4" x 23" strips, beige print, for the sashing
- Cut 9: 8" squares, beige to brown prints, for the background squares
- Cut 2: 1 1/2" x 26 1/2" strips, dark brown solid, for the border
- Cut 2: 1 1/2" x 25" strips, dark brown solid, for the border
- Cut 4: 2 1/2" x 44" strips, dark brown solid, for the binding
- Cut 9: 8" squares of tear-away stabilizer

DIRECTIONS

- Referring to *Basic Steps to Making Cutout Quilts* (page 4) make the 9 Casey's Friends blocks. Appliqué the dark brown eyes in place.
- Remove the stabilizer.
- Lay out a 2 1/4" x 23" beige print strip. Arrange 2 bones alternately with 3 puppy dog motifs on the strip, beginning and ending with the puppy dogs. Refer to the photo as necessary. Fuse the appliqués in place according to the manufacturer's instructions to make a sashing. Make 2.
- Referring to the quilt photo, lay out the Casey's Friends blocks alternately with the sashings.
- Stitch the blocks into rows. Join the rows and sashing.
- Stitch the 1 1/2" x 26 1/2" dark brown solid strips to the sides of the quilt.
- Stitch the 1 1/2" x 25" dark brown solid strips to the top and bottom of the quilt.
- Outline embroider (page 6) the details of the dogs' faces. Use beige floss for darker dogs and brown floss for lighter dogs. Use red floss for the satin stitched tongues.
- Quilt as desired and use the 2 1/2" x 44" dark brown solid strips for the binding.

Pattern for Casey's Friends
(Enlarge by 200%)
(Additional patterns on page 29)

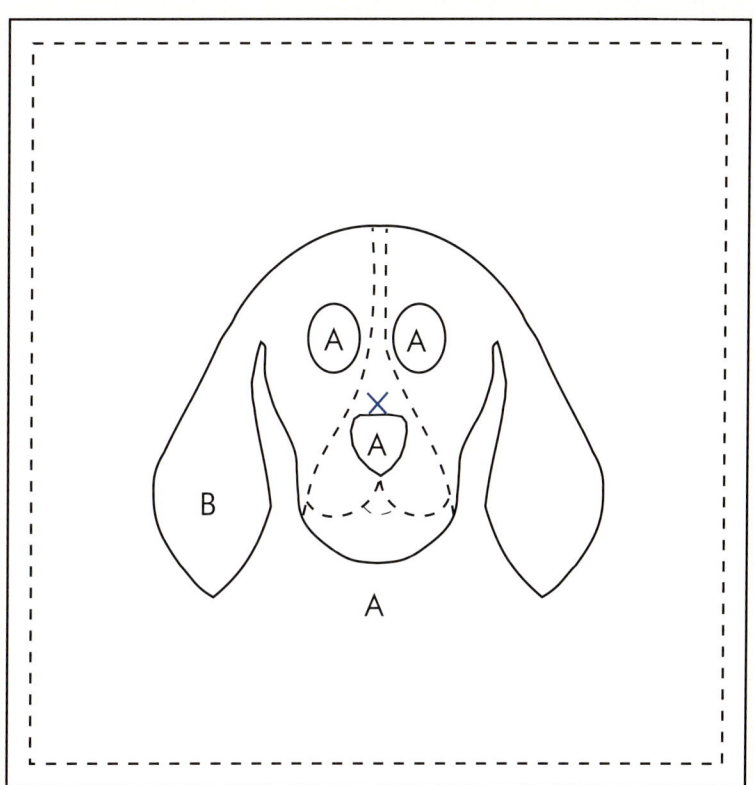

Starfish in the Lagoon

Take a fantasy trip to the tropics and stitch starfish.

*The lovely turquoise, green, and purple colors of the stars in **"Starfish in the Lagoon"** reminded me of magical starfish in a tropical lagoon. The lattice appliquéd sashing strips contribute design lines that twist and turn a little bit around the blocks.*

QUILT SIZE: 39" x 51"
BLOCK SIZE: 10" square

MATERIALS

- 6 assorted blue, violet, green, and turquoise prints, each at least 8 1/2" square, for the appliqué blocks
- 12 assorted blue, violet, green, and turquoise prints, each at least 10 1/2" square, for the background squares
- 1 1/2 yards rose print, for the sashing, border, and binding
- 3/4 yard red violet print, for the lattice strips
- 1 5/8 yards backing fabric
- 44" x 56" piece of batting
- Paper backed fusible web
- Tear-away stabilizer
- 4 pattern copies (See *Basic Steps to Making Cutout Quilts* on page 4.)
- Basting spray
- 1/4" bias press bar

CUTTING

Enlarge the pattern on page 28 by 200%. Dimensions given include a 1/4" seam allowance. Cut lengthwise strips before cutting other pieces from the same yardage.

For the appliqués:
Prepare the following squares for this Style 2 project with the fusible web as described in Basic Steps to Making Cutout Quilts *on page 4.*

- Cut 6: 8 1/2" squares, assorted blue, violet, green, and turquoise prints

Also:

- Cut 12: 10 1/2" squares, assorted blue, violet, green and turquoise prints, for the background squares
- Cut 4: 2 1/2" x 50 1/2" lengthwise strips, rose print, for the binding
- Cut 2: 2 1/2" x 50 1/2" lengthwise strips, rose print, for the border
- Cut 2: 2 1/2" x 34 1/2" lengthwise strips, rose print, for the border
- Cut 17: 2 1/2" x 10 1/2" strips, rose print, for the sashings
- Cut 6: 2 1/2" squares, rose print, for the cornerstones
- Cut 18: 1" x 32" bias strips, red violet print, for the lattice strips
- Cut 12: 10 1/2" squares of tear-away stabilizer

DIRECTIONS

- Referring to *Basic Steps to Making Cutout Quilts* (page 4), make the 12 Starfish in the Lagoon blocks.
- Remove the stabilizer.

For the latticed sashings:

- Fold a 1" x 33" red violet bias strip in half lengthwise, wrong side in. Stitch 1/4" from the cut edges, making a long tube. Trim the seam allowance to 1/8".
- Slip the 1/4" bias press bar into the tube. Gently twist the fabric tube until the seam lies along the center of the bar. If the tube is too tight, adjust the seam allowance. Press the seam to one side. A little steam will aid in setting the seam.
- Slide the bar a little further into the tube and continue pressing until the entire tube is pressed. Remove the bar when the fabric has cooled. Repeat this process for 8 tubes.
- Transfer the placement lines for the bias lattices from the pattern on page 28 to the 2 1/2" x 10 1/2" rose print sashing strips. Appliqué the prepared bias strips in place. Make 17. Set them aside.

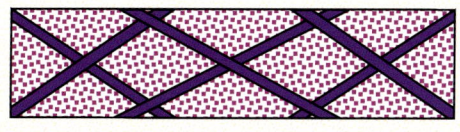

- In the same manner, appliqué bias strips to a 2 1/2" rose print cornerstone square. Make 6.

- Lay out 3 sashing strips alternately with 2 cornerstone squares. Stitch them together to make a pieced sashing. Make 3.
- Referring to the quilt photo for placement, lay out the blocks in 4 rows of 3, alternately with the remaining 2 1/2" x 10 1/2" lattice sashings. Place the pieced sashings between the rows.
- Stitch the blocks and lattice sashings into rows.
- Join the block rows and pieced sashings to make the quilt top.
- Stitch the 2 1/2" x 34 1/2" rose print strips to the top and bottom of the quilt.
- Stitch the 2 1/2" x 50 1/2" rose print strips to the sides of the quilt.
- Quilt as desired and use the 2 1/2" x 50 1/2" rose print strips for the binding.

Hearts

Celebrate Valentine's Day with a new twist!

*"**Hearts**" is a very quick and easy project and makes a thoughtful Valentine's Day gift or wall quilt. Embroidered lazy daisy flowers add a nice touch, but you could embellish this charming quilt any way you wish.*

QUILT SIZE: 25" x 31"
BLOCK SIZE: 6" square

MATERIALS

- 10 assorted red and pink prints, each at least 5" square, for the appliqués
- 20 assorted gray prints, each at least 6 1/2" square, for the background squares
- 1/3 yard red print for the binding
- 1 yard backing fabric
- 29" x 35" square piece of batting
- Paper backed fusible web
- Tear-away stabilizer
- 5 pattern copies (See *Basic Steps to Making Cutout Quilts* on page 4.)
- Basting spray
- 2 yards of 4 mm. red silk ribbon for the lazy daisy flowers

CUTTING
Enlarge the pattern by 200%. Dimensions given include a 1/4" seam allowance.

For the appliqués:
Prepare the following squares for this Style 2 project with the fusible web as described in Basic Steps to Making Cutout Quilts *on page 4.*

- Cut 10: 5" squares, assorted red and pink prints

Also:
- Cut 20: 6 1/2" squares, assorted gray prints, for the background squares
- Cut 4: 2 1/2" x 44" strips, red print, for the binding
- Cut 20: 6 1/2" squares of tear-away stabilizer

DIRECTIONS

- Referring to *Basic Steps to Making Cutout Quilts* (page 4) make the 20 Heart blocks.
- Remove the stabilizer.
- Referring to the quilt photo for placement, lay out the Heart blocks in 4 rows of 5. Sew them into rows and join the rows.
- Make Lazy Daisy stitches (page 6) at the intersections of the blocks with the 4 mm. red silk ribbon.
- Quilt as desired and use the 2 1/2" x 44" red print strips for the binding.

Pattern for Hearts
(Enlarge by 200%)

Curvaceous Curves

Use rich colors for this elegant, contemporary quilt.

"Curvaceous Squares" *was stitched and quilted by Susan Marsh. An elegant looking quilt in rich colors, this would be perfect in any room. The color combinations in the quilt on page 19 would be wonderful in a child's room.*

QUILT SIZE: 42" square
BLOCK SIZE: 10" square

MATERIALS

- Green tone-on-tone print, at least 8 1/2" square
- Purple tone-on-tone print, at least 8 1/2" x 17"
- Fat quarter (18" x 22") red tone-on-tone print
- 1 yard light floral for the background blocks
- 1 1/4 yards dark green print for the border, sashing, and binding
- 46" square of backing fabric
- 46" square piece of batting
- Paper backed fusible web
- Tear-away stabilizer
- 3 pattern copies (See *Basic Steps to Making Cutout Quilts* on page 4.)
- Basting spray

CUTTING

Enlarge the pattern on page 29 by 200%. Dimensions given include a 1/4" seam allowance.

For the appliqués:

Prepare the following squares for this Style 2 project with the fusible web as described in Basic Steps to Making Cutout Quilts *on page 4.*

- Cut 1: 8 1/2" square, green tone-on-tone print
- Cut 2: 8 1/2" squares, purple tone-on-tone print
- Cut 2: 8 1/2" squares, red tone-on-tone print

Also:

- Cut 4: 3 1/2" squares, red tone-on-tone print, for the cornerstones
- Cut 9: 10 1/2" squares, light floral
- Cut 4: 2 1/2" x 44" strips, dark green print, for the binding
- Cut 6: 3 1/2" x 36 1/2" strips, dark green print, for the vertical sashings and border
- Cut 6: 3 1/2" x 10 1/2" strips, dark green print, for the horizontal sashings
- Cut 9: 10 1/2" squares of tear-away stabilizer

DIRECTIONS

- Referring to *Basic Steps to Making Cutout Quilts* (page 4), make the 9 Curvaceous Squares blocks.
- Remove the stabilizer.
- Referring to the quilt photo for placement, lay out the blocks in 3 vertical rows of 3, alternately with the 3 1/2" x 10 1/2" dark green horizontal sashings. Place the 3 1/2" x 36 1/2" dark green vertical sashings between the rows.
- Stitch the blocks and horizontal sashings into rows. Join the rows and vertical sashings.
- Stitch two 3 1/2" x 36 1/2" dark green print strips to opposite sides of the quilt.
- Stitch a 3 1/2" red tone-on-tone print square to each end of the remaining 3 1/2" x 36 1/2" dark green print strips. Stitch them to the remaining sides of the quilt.
- Quilt as desired and use the 2 1/2" x 44" dark green print strips for the binding.

This version of **"Curvaceous Squares"** *uses bright colors and contains 12 blocks with no sashing strips.*

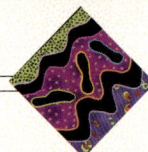

Zigzag

Bright colors spark this playful quilt.

*Lively squiggles and noodles playfully scoot across the surface of **"Zigzag"**. The colors become vivid on a black background and the diagonal stripes of the borders shout, "Wow!!! Look at me!"*

QUILT SIZE: 27" square
BLOCK SIZE: 6" square

MATERIALS

- 5 assorted bright prints, each at least 6 1/2" square, for the appliqués
- 1 yard black solid for the background squares, inner border and binding
- Assorted bright prints, each at least 1 1/2" x 22" for the outer border
- 1 yard backing fabric
- 33" square piece of batting
- Paper backed fusible web
- Tear-away stabilizer
- 3 pattern copies (See *Basic Steps to Making Cutout Quilts* on page 4.)
- Basting spray

CUTTING

Enlarge the pattern by 200%. Dimensions given include a 1/4" seam allowance.

For the appliqués:

Prepare the following squares for this Style 1 project with the fusible web as described in Basic Steps to Making Cutout Quilts *on page 4.*

- Cut 5: 6 1/2" squares, assorted bright prints

Also:

- Cut 9: 6 1/2" squares, black solid, for the background squares
- Cut 2: 1 1/2" x 18 1/2" strips, black solid, for the inner border
- Cut 2: 1 1/2" x 20 1/2" strips, black solid, for the inner border
- Cut 3: 2 1/2" x 44" strips, black solid, for the binding
- Cut 20: 1 1/2" x 22" strips, bright prints, for the outer border
- Cut 9: 6 1/2" squares of tear-away stabilizer

DIRECTIONS

- Referring to *Basic Steps to Making Cutout Quilts* (page 4) make the 9 Zigzag blocks.
- Remove the stabilizer.
- Referring to the quilt photo for placement, lay out the Zigzag blocks in 3 rows of 3.
- Stitch the blocks into rows and join the rows.
- Stitch the 1 1/2" x 18 1/2" black solid strips to opposite sides of the quilt.
- Stitch the 1 1/2" x 20 1/2" black solid strips to the remaining sides of the quilt.
- Stitch two 1 1/2" x 22" bright print strips right sides together along their length to make a pieced panel, offsetting strips by 1", as shown.

- Stitch additional 1 1/2" x 22" bright print strips to the pieced panel until all 20 strips are incorporated.
- For the outer borders, cut four 3"-wide strips from the pieced panel.

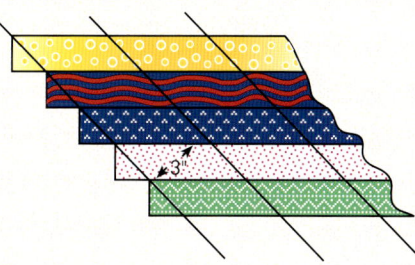

- Trim 2 borders to 3" x 20 1/2" and stitch them to opposite sides of the quilt.
- Trim 2 borders to 25 1/2" and stitch them to the remaining sides of the quilt.
- Quilt as desired and use the 2 1/2" x 44" black solid strips for the binding.

Pattern for Zigzag
(Enlarge by 200%)

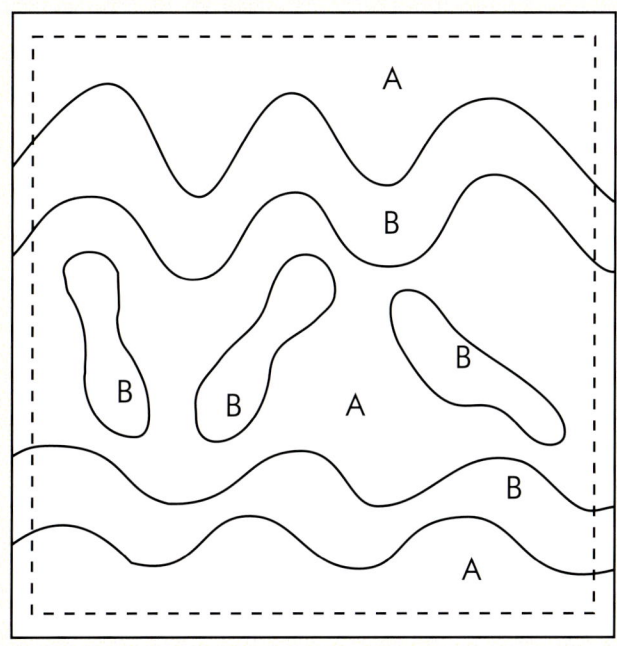

Flower Garden

Groom your green thumb without breaking ground.

Grow your own flower garden in a quilt, then place it in your sunroom, kitchen, or other sunny place. **"Flower Garden"** *is an easy place to cultivate your best efforts. And you won't have to worry about the bugs, because they're friendly!*

QUILT SIZE: 29" square
BLOCK SIZE: 7 1/2" square

MATERIALS

- 5 assorted red and blue prints, each at least 6 1/2" square, for the appliqués
- 9 assorted light green, blue, and yellow prints, each at least 8" square, for the background squares
- 1/2 yard red tone-on-tone print for the inner border and binding
- 1/4 yard each of pale yellow and bright blue prints for the outer border
- Scraps of an insect print with at least 4 complete motifs
- 1 yard backing fabric
- 35" square of batting
- Paper backed fusible web
- Tear-away stabilizer
- 3 pattern copies (See *Basic Steps to Making Cutout Quilts* on page 4.)
- Basting spray

CUTTING

Enlarge the pattern by 200%. Dimensions given include a 1/4" seam allowance.

For the appliqués:
Prepare the following squares for this Style 2 project with the fusible web as described in Basic Steps to Making Cutout Quilts *on page 4.*

- Cut 5: 6 1/2" squares, assorted red and blue prints

Also:

- Cut 9: 8" squares, assorted light green, blue, and yellow prints, for the background squares
- Cut 2: 1 1/4" x 23" strips, red tone-on-tone print, for the inner border
- Cut 2: 1 1/4" x 24 1/2" strips, red tone-on-tone print, for the inner border
- Cut 3: 2 1/2" x 44" strips, red tone-on-tone print, for the binding
- Cut 3: 1 1/2" x 44" strips, yellow print, for the outer border
- Cut 3: 1 1/2" x 44" strips, bright blue print, for the outer order
- Cut 4: 2 7/8" squares, pale yellow print, then cut them in half diagonally, to yield 8 triangles
- Cut 4: 2 7/8" squares, insect print, then cut them in half diagonally to yield 8 triangles
- Cut 9: 8" squares of tear-away stabilizer

DIRECTIONS

- Referring to *Basic Steps to Making Cutout Quilts* (page 4) make the 9 Flower Garden blocks.
- Remove the stabilizer.
- Referring to the quilt photo for placement, lay out the Flower Garden blocks in 3 rows of 3.
- Stitch the blocks into rows and join the rows.
- Stitch the 1 1/4" x 23" red tone-on-tone print strips to the top and bottom of the quilt.
- Stitch the 1 1/4" x 24 1/2" red tone-on-tone print strips to the sides of the quilt.

For the outer border:

- Stitch a 1 1/2" x 44" pale yellow print strip to a 1 1/2" x 44" bright blue print strip, right sides together, along their length to make a pieced panel. Make 3.

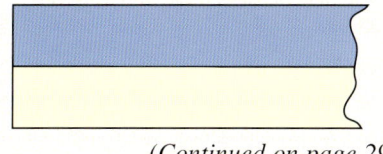

(Continued on page 29)

Pattern for Flower Garden
(Enlarge by 200%)

Giraffes on Parade

Bright and perky, these little critters march to the beat of their own drum!

"Giraffes on Parade" looks bright and happy hanging on a wall in a child's bedroom. The button eyes can be embroidered if a child will use this quilt to cuddle up in.

QUILT SIZE: 28 1/2" square
BLOCK SIZE: 7" square

MATERIALS

- 5 assorted medium and bright prints, each at least 6" square, for the appliqués
- 9 assorted light prints for the background squares
- 2/3 yard purple print, each at least 7 1/2" square, for the sashing, border, and binding
- 6" square green print for the cornerstones
- 1 yard backing fabric
- 33" square piece of batting
- Assorted colors of embroidery floss
- Nine 3/16" black buttons, for the giraffe's eyes (NOTE: *For safety reasons, if a young child will use this quilt, embroider the eyes with a satin stitch in place of the buttons.*)
- 3 packages of variegated jumbo rickrack
- Paper backed fusible web
- Tear-away stabilizer
- 3 pattern copies (See *Basic Steps to Making Cutout Quilts* on page 4.)
- Basting spray

CUTTING

Enlarge the pattern by 200%. Dimensions given include a 1/4" seam allowance.

For the appliqués:

Prepare the following squares for this Style 2 project with the fusible web as described in Basic Steps to Making Cutout Quilts *on page 4.*

- Cut 5: 6" squares, assorted medium and bright prints

Also:

- Cut 9: 7 1/2" squares, light prints, for the background squares
- 12: 2" x 7 1/2" strips, purple print, for the sashing
- Cut 4: 2" squares, green print, for the cornerstones
- Cut 2: 2" x 24 1/2" strips, purple print, for the border
- Cut 2: 2" x 27 1/2" strips, purple print, for the border
- Cut 3: 2 1/2" x 44" strips, purple print, for the binding
- Cut 12: 8" lengths, variegated jumbo rickrack
- Cut 9: 7 1/2" squares of tear-away stabilizer
- Cut 2: 26" strips variegated jumbo rickrack
- Cut 2: 29" strips, variegated jumbo rickrack

DIRECTIONS

- Referring to *Basic Steps to Making Cutout Quilts* (page 4) make the 9 Giraffes on Parade blocks.
- Remove the stabilizer.
- Stitch 3/16" black buttons in place for the eyes, or, if you prefer, embroider the eyes with black embroidery floss and satin stitches.
- To make a giraffe's tail, cut 6" lengths from 7 different colors of embroidery floss.
- Place all 7 pieces together and tie a knot close to one end.
- Sew the tail in place through the knot. Trim the tail to 2 /14".
- Make tails for the remaining Giraffes on Parade blocks in the same manner.

(Continued on page 29.)

Pattern for Giraffes on Parade
(Enlarge by 200%)

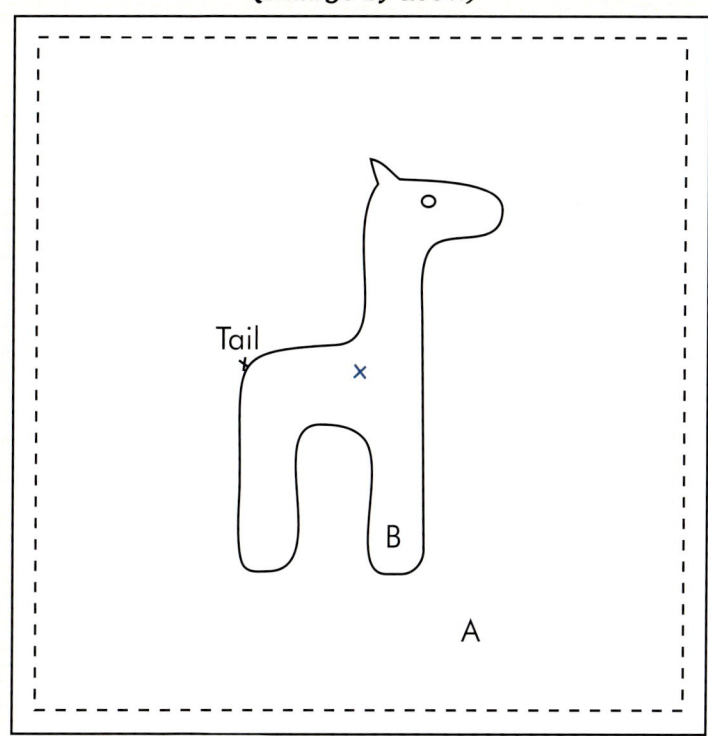

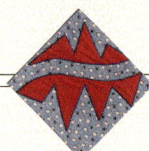

Jagged Edges

Streaks of lightening appear to bolt through this quilt.

*I chose to use patriotic colors and reproduction prints for my version of **"Jagged Edges"**. The muted colors give the quilt a look that blends nicely with a country decorating theme.*

QUILT SIZE: 29" square
BLOCK SIZE: 8" square

MATERIALS
- 5 assorted blue and red prints, each at least 8 1/2" square, for the appliqués
- 3/4 yard navy print for the background squares and binding
- 1/3 yard red solid
- 1/2 yard stripe print for the borders
- 6" square, blue stripe for the cornerstones
- 1 yard backing fabric
- 34" square of batting
- Paper backed fusible web
- Tear-away stabilizer
- 3 pattern copies (See *Basic Steps to Making Cutout Quilts* on page 4.)
- Basting spray

CUTTING
Enlarge the pattern by 200%. Dimensions given include a 1/4" seam allowance.

For the appliqués:
Prepare the following squares for this Style 1 project with the fusible web as described in Basic Steps to Making Cutout Quilts *on page 4.*
- Cut 5: 8 1/2" squares, assorted blue and red prints

Also cut:
- Cut 5: 8 1/2" squares, navy print, for background squares
- Cut 4: 8 1/2" squares, red solid
- Cut 4: 2 1/2" x 24 1/2" crosswise strips, stripe, for the borders
- Cut 4: 2 1/2" squares, blue stripe, for the cornerstones
- Cut 4: 2 1/2" x 44" strips, navy print, for the binding
- Cut 9: 8 1/2" squares of tear-away stabilizer

DIRECTIONS
- Referring to *Basic Steps to Making Cutout Quilts* (page 4) make 9 Jagged Edges blocks.
- Remove the stabilizer.
- Referring to the quilt photo for placement, lay out the Jagged Edges blocks in 3 rows of 3.
- Stitch the blocks into rows and join the rows.
- Stitch two 2 1/2"x 24 1/2" stripe strips to opposite sides of the quilt.
- Stitch a 2 1/2" blue stripe square to each end of a remaining 2 1/2" x 24 1/2" stripe strip to make a pieced border. Make 2.
- Stitch the pieced borders to the remaining sides of the quilt.
- Quilt as desired and use the 2 1/2" x 44" navy print strips for the binding.

Tip:
When selecting thread for machine appliqué, you may choose a color that blends with either the background square or the cutout. For greater definition of the pattern, use a thread that contrasts with both the background and the cutout.

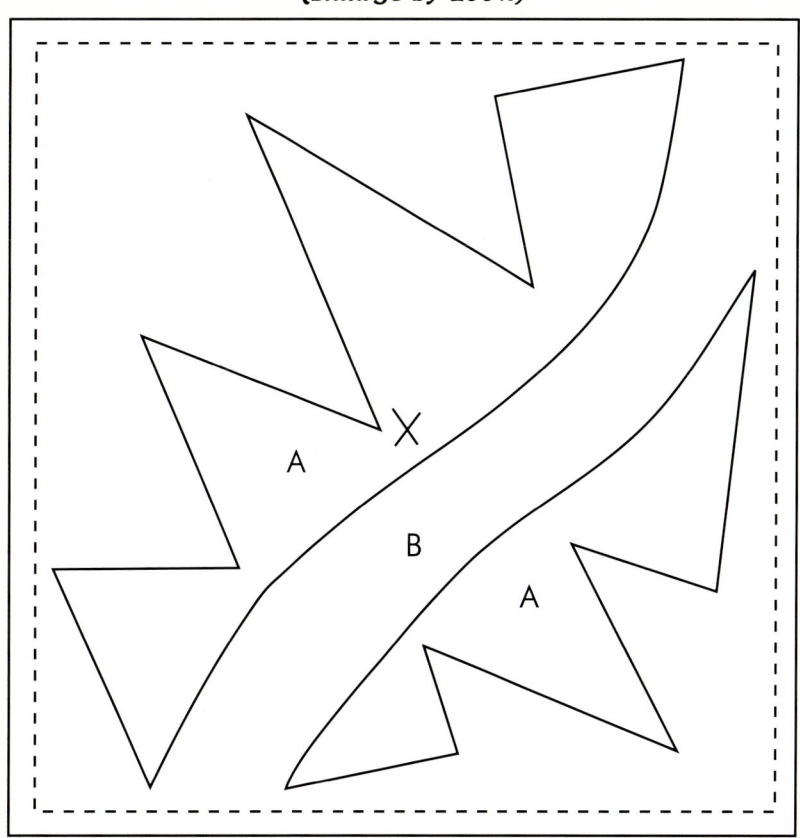

Pattern for Jagged Edges
(Enlarge by 200%)

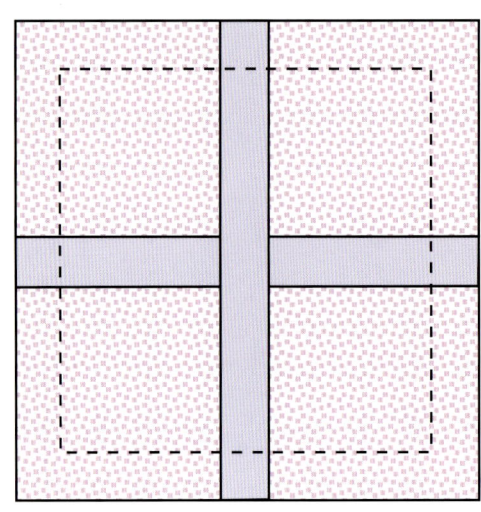

Pattern for Starfish in the Lagoon
(Enlarge by 200%)
(Instructions begin on page 15)

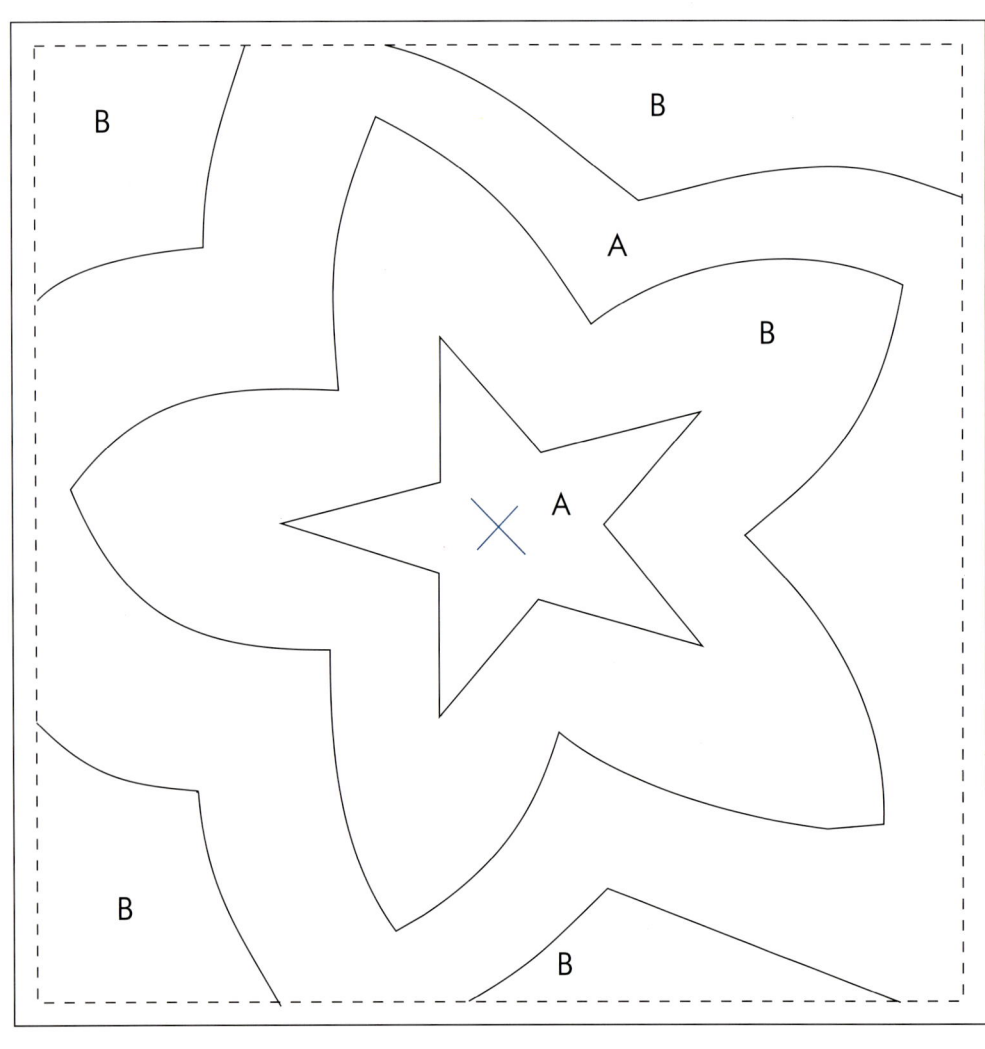
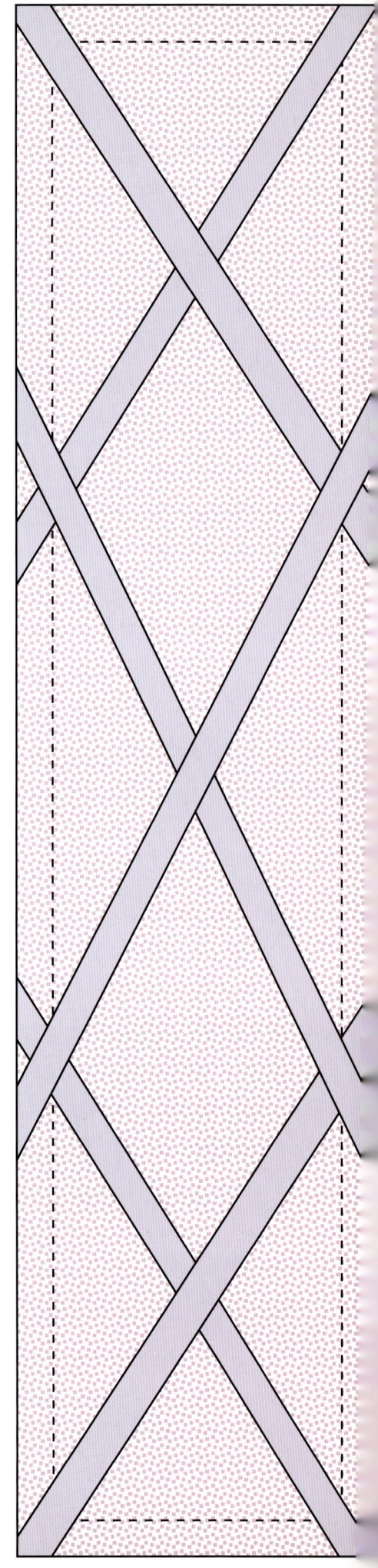

Patterns for Casey's Friends
(Instructions begin on page 13)

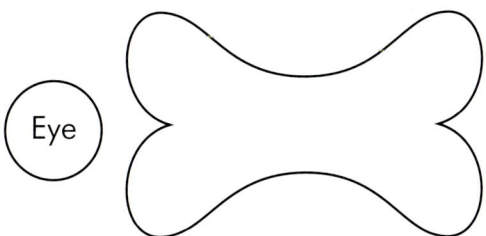

Flower Garden
(continued from page 23)

- Cut eighty 1 1/2" sections from the pieced panels, as shown.

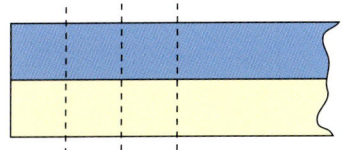

- Lay out 20 sections and 2 yellow outer border triangles, as shown, and stitch them together to make a pieced border. Make 4.

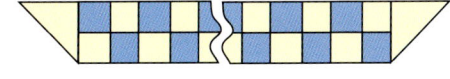

- Stitch a pieced border to each side of the quilt.
- Stitch a bug fabric square to each end of the remaining borders. Sew them to the top and bottom.
- Quilt as desired and use the 2 1/2" x 44" red tone-on-tone print strips for the binding.

Giraffes on Parade
(continued from page 25)

- Embroider around the giraffes with an outline stitch. (NOTE: *See the instructions for embroidery stitches on page 6.*)
- Center and topstitch an 8" length of variegated jumbo rickrack on a 2" x 7 1/2" purple print strip to make a sashing. Make 12.
- Trim the ends of the rickrack even with the ends of the sashings.
- In the same manner, stitch rickrack to two 2" x 24 1/2" and two 2" x 27 1/2" purple print border strips. Trim the ends of the rickrack even with the ends of the border strips. Set them aside.
- Lay out three 2" x 7 1/2" sashings alternately with two 2" green print squares. Stitch them together to make a sashing row. Make 2.
- Referring to the quilt photo on page 24 for placement, lay out the blocks in 3 rows of 3 alternating them with the remaining 7 1/2" sashings.
- Stitch the blocks and sashings into rows.
- Join the block rows and sashing rows.
- Stitch the 2" x 24 1/2" border strips to opposite sides of the quilt.
- Stitch the 2" x 27 1/2" border strips to the remaining sides of the quilt.
- Quilt as desired and use the 2 1/2" x 44" purple print strips for the binding.

Pattern for Curvaceous Squares
(Enlarge by 200%)
(Instructions begins on page 19)

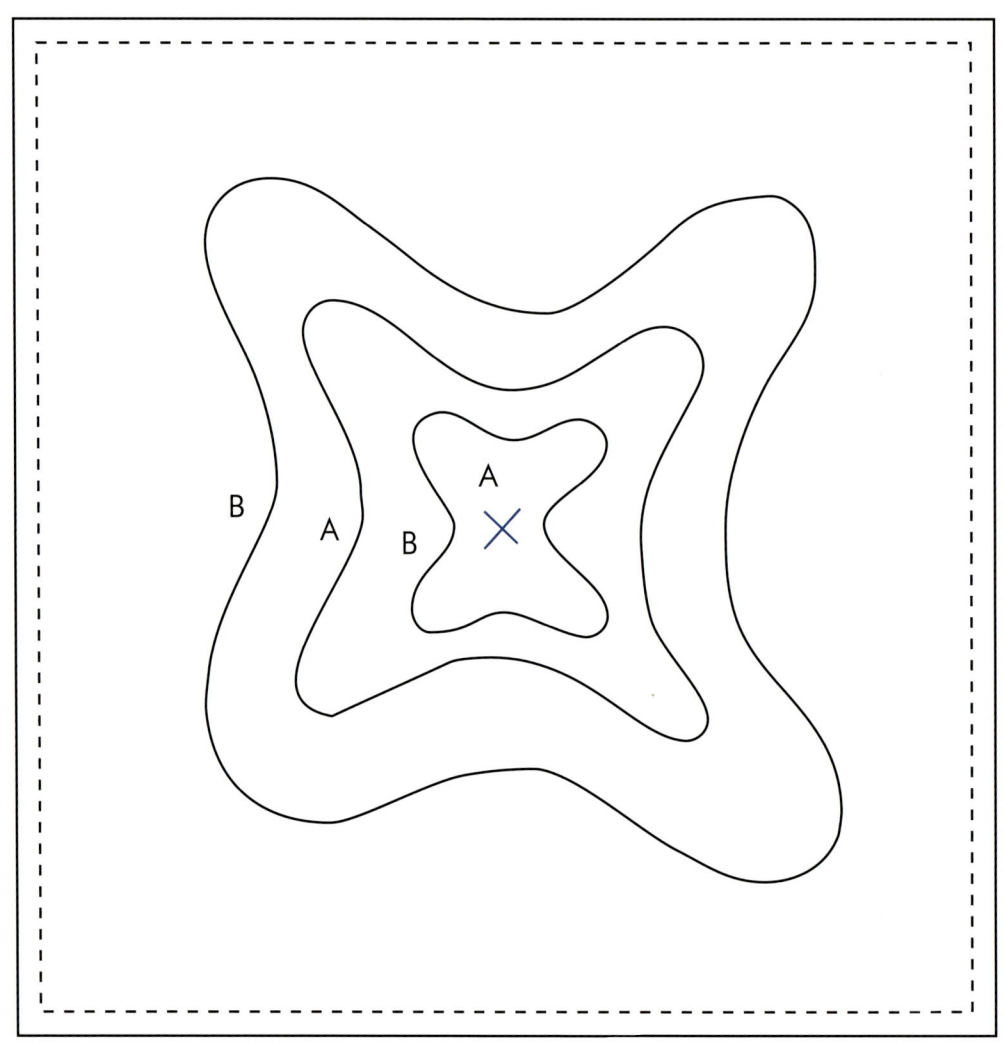

Bonus Designs!

Pattern for Flying High
(Enlarge by 200%)

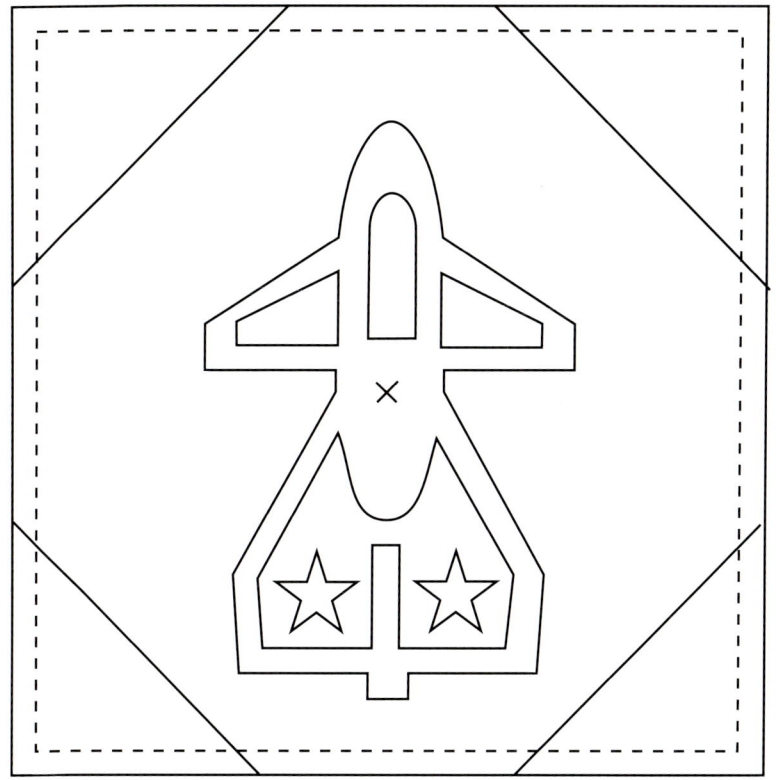

Flying High

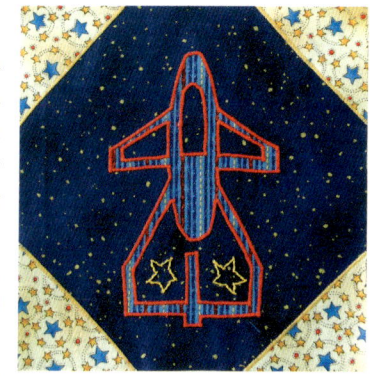

This is a fun design for young children or maybe even adults who love airplanes. I think it looks nice in patriotic colors of red, white, and blue. I used a small-scale star print and a stripe among other selections and placed the planes on a dark blue background to represent the night sky. The stars are embroidered on the background in any color thread that stands out on your plane or background fabric. Cut 8" squares for the background blocks and appliqué blocks. This is a Style 1 project.

Pattern for Pop Music
(Enlarge by 200%)

Pop Music

A guitar and musical notes are just right for a teenager who loves music. Select bright colors for the appliqués and background fabrics. The dark areas on the pattern indicate that you can add a machine-sewn satin stitch on the negative (cutout block) variation of the block. This adds a little more definition to the design. Cut 8" squares for the background blocks and appliqué blocks. This is a Style 1 project.

Bonus Design!

Pattern for Quilter's Delight
(Enlarge by 200%)

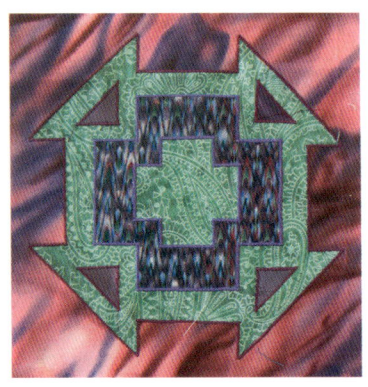

Quilter's Delight
This quilt block design is a perfect project for any lover of quilts. Select colors to fit any decor, from elegant to country. Cut 10 1/2" squares for the background and appliqué blocks. This is a Style 1 project.